I Vote and I Deplore Politicians

by

John Farrow

Gotham Books

30 N Gould St.
Ste. 20820, Sheridan, WY 82801
https://gothambooksinc.com/

Phone: 1 (307) 464-7800

© 2023 *John Farrow*. All rights reserved.

No part of this book may be reproduced, stored in a retrieval system, or transmitted by any means without the written permission of the author.

Published by Gotham Books (June 1, 2023)

ISBN: 979-8-88775-254-9 (P)
ISBN: 979-8-88775-255-6 (E)
ISBN: 979-8-88775-256-3 (H)

Because of the dynamic nature of the Internet, any web addresses or links contained in this book may have changed since publication and may no longer be valid.

The views expressed in this work are solely those of the author and do not necessarily reflect the views of the publisher, and the publisher hereby disclaims any responsibility for them.

Table of Contents

Introduction 1

Chapter 1 17

Chapter 2 33

Chapter 3 40

Chapter 4 59

Chapter 5 63

Chapter 6 69

Chapter 7 73

Prologue 84

About The Author 93

WHEN DO YOUNG PEOPLE BEGIN TO LOOK
AND REALIZE "THE DREAMING TREE"
A REFLECTION INTO THEIR FUTURE IS DYING?

Introduction

When asking myself why should I care what happens in America, our family's homeland for over five generations and the irreversible destruction we are causing to Planet Earth, knowing the time I've spent during this truly magical mystery tour of life, where my dreams and ambitions have been fulfilled beyond most people's wildest imagination, now makes my journey in this realm of existence feel complete! But that's not who I am and while raised to believe that everyone has a moral responsibility to one another, especially our children and future generations, would hope as you read through the passages to follow, it provides a wakeup call in your human psyche asking if you too are concerned about the untold challenges mankind faces today when we as a society remain silent in complicity, with so many uncertainties now causing pause in people's lives to ever try and move forward again. Those seemingly immovable roadblocks alongside the greatest threat to all humanity now rising above all other perilous risks being taken for all life on the planet to merely exist long-term in a more hostile environment through global warming, should make everyone mindful, especially parents, of what we're leaving behind for the truly innocent members of society to try and navigate through on their own!

The inconvenient truth moves further into the forefront of everyone's lives today, knowing we all should have acted sooner to manage the errors in judgement being made in our past instead of trying to deflect the truth by blaming others for the dire position America and the planet rests in today! While I remain confident that positive changes are still attainable, time is truly running out to try and correct the damage we've already caused to the country, the planet and people's lives without immediate and actionable solutions found by those responsible for creating most of what remains wrong in America today. Sound bites and empty rhetoric continuing to come out of Washington alongside redundant and superfluous reporting by most news media outlets will remain a distraction in most people's minds before Mother Earth finally steps in to decide the future fate of all life on the planet through the irreversible damage we've already caused to the environment while ignoring the urgency mankind has to slow global warming sooner than later for the future of humanity!

I was taught at a young age to believe in the role our elected leaders swore an oath in guaranteeing unlimited protection to every man, woman and child on American soil whenever our health, wellbeing and security became threatened, as it remains today throughout everyone's lives. Sadly though, as people watch in great dismay while those, we have always placed our unlimited trust in to honor their commitments they've made to the American people and performance of the Constitutional duties they swore to uphold while in office, have once again decided to turn their backs on each of us during this most crucial time of need so many now find themselves in, through no fault of our own!

I truly believe most Americans like myself have grown tired of waiting in hopeful anticipation that after the next election cycle we will finally have a majority of leaders who can then act responsibly, with a sense of morality and ethical competence to address the misguided decisions they alone have made in the past and finally begin to do what is right for their constituents and all Americans first! But as I have closely observed over the past half century, unless changes are made to the core cause behind what has now become a dysfunctional form of governance in America today, the country's pathway forward will continue to be derailed by the growing challenges ahead, before any options remaining to try and reverse course we exist on today, will then be out of our reach to act in time!

The letters and messages I've now sent to President Biden defines a clear pathway ahead for America that he alone can provide through the progressive ideas I've always envisioned for this country as our homeland, to continue along a more harmonious pathway into a more perfect union. Then, alongside the support granted him by the majority of citizens in the last election, asking that this administration begin resurrecting our now dismantled democracy with safeguards put in place so the nation can find hope once again that we will never fall into such disharmony and distrust among our fellow Americans again, the country will finally move forward again never looking back on the most insecure position it lies in today! As we all wait in hopeful anticipation for some direction or guidance coming from our leaders in Washington to try and chart a more unified and progressive pathway forward again, time is truly running out to try and instill greater hope in people's minds that a brighter future can still ahead, when most Americans have seen little to no improvements in their own lives yet to be realized. I have shown in my suggestions now sent to the Oval Office, practical non-partisan solutions this president can put into practice quickly without the need for Congresses approval, so leadership can begin thinking outside the status quo mentality driving Washington's counterproductive decisions, that continue to take the nation in the wrong direction today. President Biden must begin to start taking the necessary risks going forward, focusing on ways to try and overcome the almost insurmountable challenges the country still faces today, when future Federal Elections, National Security Threats, Gun Violence, Income Inequality, Student Debt, Access to Healthcare for Everyone, Immigration Reform and Civil Unrest will then become less of a distraction in people's lives so leaders in Washington can then move to focus their undivided attention on the greatest threat now being made to all life on the planet. Then and only then can we become better prepared for the future fate of humanity when finding ways to sustain all life on the planet as long as possible so the human race will adapt more securely to the growing destruction throughout the environment that we must all now try and navigate through safely on our own!

It is a documented fact when other governments, framed alongside the vision that our American Republic was conceived, first focus on the health, safety and wellbeing of its citizens, then human interests rise above all else as people coexist alongside one another more harmoniously. Less crime and discontentment is reported in their communities because people's basic needs are met and maintained under an atmosphere of equity for all. This is the model of governance the founders always intended for America, protecting and serving the needs of citizens first, while evolving through the changing times ahead in a more perfect union, guided first and foremost through the Voice and Will of the People. I have lived my entire life in America under the promise made by the founders with Life, Liberty and The Pursuit of Happiness being the guideposts all citizens still have before them today, to begin experiencing life fully without further delay, knowing we're only given the opportunity to do so, once in this lifetime on planet Earth!

I continue to speak out as a lone crusader against the continued dysfunction in Washington today through the petitions started and websites I've managed, advocating for greater support from the American people when speaking out, telling President Biden the status quo mentality that leadership maintains today, is outdated and ineffective in deciding on ways to permanently remedy the growing challenges we still face in all our lives as we move further into uncharted territory day by day. With the perilous uncertainties now shaping everyone's lives one day at a time, demands mankind begin thinking outside the box for answers before Mother Earth soon closes the lid on all humanity and nailing it shut, for global warming to then determine the future fate of all life on the planet from that day forward!

The non-partisan procedural changes I've now suggested to the president awaiting his implementation into the bylaws of the Federal Government can be authorized through an Executive Order that finally begins the long awaited transformation process throughout Washington where every member of Congress is then put on notice requiring they return to the job requirements shown in the Constitution, within a bi-partisan collaborative work environment to begin addressing the growing challenges ahead without any further delays! Unfortunately, though, as a lone voice for change, any suggestions I have sent will never reach the Oval Office until We the People stand in solidarity to tell this president: Now Is the Time for His Undivided Attention to Be Focused on The Pulse of The Nation Before the Heart, Soul and Spirit of America Becomes Diminished Beyond Recognition! Otherwise, I believe it may be time to accept in the new world order we now live in stasis, that the distrust and division everyone feels towards one another will be further manipulated only to benefit a few at the cost of bringing America and people's lives further into harm's way with no direction or guidance from Washington to provide a more secure pathway forward again, especially for those who still have hopes and dreams towards a brighter future ahead in their lives yet to be lived fully!

With the societal attitudes and norms still in a transition phase after people's lives and livelihoods were placed in suspension during the pandemic, requires more than ever that we come together now and decide as one nation, one culture, to find real solutions that provide a more secure way for us all to adapt in the new world order we now live day by day, knowing everyone is in this together and no longer alone to try and emerge as a more unified nation to overcome as one, the untold challenges that still lie ahead.

With the mental health crisis rising throughout our country today where every man, woman and child needs greater assurances from leaders in Washington that they will work alongside the people to provide those in need the resources required, especially for young people who are now having to address the health challenges they continue to face on their own. With effective and lasting solutions still available that will start to address this underlying mental health threat people of all ages face today, mandates the current dysfunction in Washington be resolved before this president can then focus solely on what he has always shown the American people while in public office, his moral competency to deliver on the promise made by all elected officials when guaranteeing everyone's health and wellbeing be maintained while protecting and serving the needs of all citizens first and foremost!

Then this Administration can begin working outside of public view and start to address the mental health crises alongside the professionals who have the capacity to show people of all ages how to become part of the solutions necessary in providing for their own health needs while showing others how to do so for themselves, so they can finally step away from their feelings of isolation to find greater meaning and purpose in their lives yet to be lived fully. Those already having the skills needed or want to learn what's required in starting to address the waste and redundancy throughout government, will be financially compensated from a portion of the funds they've recovered with the remainder being used to pay down the national debt. A win win scenario with no rationale for not implementing such a program into practice if it benefits those currently in mental distress and helps the country reduce its dependence on other nations we are currently indebted to with no relief in sight. The same goes for the re-enactment of the Welfare to Work Program so those still hoping to maintain a sense of dignity through a more productive lifestyle but unable to do so because of a physical disability they now have, can be trained to perform at a new task, while being paid a living wage and finding greater purpose in life by no longer contributing to Washingtons' inability to try and address the reason why the poverty conditions in America become more unmanageable year after year.

President Biden can then ask young people to pause and look into the future now with opportunities provided that will incentivize them to become part of the solutions necessary in charting a more innovative and progressive pathway forward in their own lives yet to be lived fully. Imagine the possibilities when they finally look up from the electronic devices we have all become so attached to and begin internalizing what unlimited possibilities await each of us and to unleash the curiosity most feel but unable to act upon, asking 'what if' there was a way to teleport people and carry on a conversation with one another face to face, in person once more, then being offered a position with the Space Exploration Program to begin finding ways to advance into the 21st century after 23 years with America still lying in wait, unable to move into a new era while other industrialized nations now pass us by.

There are practical non-partisan solutions I have that will begin to remedy most of what remains wrong in America without further delays, when showing how even the most grandiose visions into the future can readily be turned into reality the way I've always done throughout this engaging life of mine. President Biden can then use the resources before him and focus his undivided attention on moving the nation ahead again without the needless interruptions and delays always coming out of Washington to distract people's attention away from the critical work that still needs to be done now. Then the work being performed by lawmakers will remain in the background of people's lives so we can begin to choose our own direction forward again without waiting another day for leadership to tell us how or when to start doing so on our own!

So, let's focus for a moment on the difference between debating an idea and implementing that idea into practice. Many scholars and specialists in their fields of expertise understand the importance of a collaborative discussion when presenting the pros and cons of an idea before it is implemented and put into practice. Unless some individuals present in the debate have physic powers to see into the future, the final outcome of an idea can only truly be determined once implemented and put to the test in a real-time environment. I personally have accomplished so much in my life already, not by speculating what if, but by trying out the ideas I've internalized in my mind to find the best solution as a means to an end. Mistakes will be made when acting on an idea for the first time but the real mistake in life is not even trying something because of fear of failure with the ultimate outcome. Lessons learned throughout my journey so far have always reinforced my self-esteem and purpose in life because I weighed success and failure equally. My knowledge base continued to be strengthened as my confidence in the ability to succeed at whatever I undertook grew even stronger with each challenge I undertook. Bottom line is at least I tried things to see if they were right for me and those in proximity to those endeavors, I acted upon, while always confident in my ability to fulfill my own personal expectations and more often than not, exceeding them. Challenging my curiosity into practices was far more rewarding than just engaging with the chorus of naysayers while chanting how bad an idea is before ever even tried.

It's past time to start taking greater risks in life, thinking outside the box to try and overcome the adverse conditions we live through today before someday sooner than later, when our children go outside to play they will have to wear protective suits to try and navigate in the extreme weather conditions growing more dangerous year after year, with no changes on the horizon to slow global warming except to set arbitrary dates when we will ever get started and slow the damage already done to the environment that all life must try now to adapt and survive as long as possible.

I think we should all live and practice the following mantra: **Our time on this planet is short. Life is not promised, tomorrow may not come**. Even if we don't face any major financial setbacks and remain in relatively good health, we have at most, 50-60 years of *quality time* as adults. During this period, life has to have some purpose or meaning. The most gratifying and fulfilling purpose to your life on this planet should be genuinely caring for the wellbeing of others and for yourself. As long as you have a positive impact on another human while living or after you're gone, your purpose on this planet has been, or will be fulfilled. I know I will never forget those who have touched my emotions and connected with my soul during my life so far. Unfortunately, with each new generation this connection and ability to genuinely care for another human being becomes more distant in an environment built around division and distrust towards one another as we have in America today. Perhaps because people have experienced so much pain and suffering personally or because of the number of tragedies covered by the news media on a daily basis, our human emotions have become more desensitized than ever before and leaving us unable to expend the energy remaining to focus on anyone other than ourselves.

I think some news media outlets today by promoting their commentary of fear and hatred toward others around us simply because people have different views and beliefs, have falsely created an atmosphere in this country of distrust towards our fellow citizens. I know it will never go back to the way it was but do you really want your children and grandchildren to live their lives under a belief to "do unto others, before they do unto you," or should we as a society try and advocate now and for future generations to live a more harmonious existence during the brief journey on this planet by "doing unto others as you would like to have them do unto you." I have often wondered what some of the commentators seen on conservative news shows today discuss with their children or grandchildren about family and societal values. Do these innocent youths know that those who they look up to and trust for their contribution towards a compassionate and caring environment for them to grow up in, are directly responsible for the continued decay of moral values seen around the world today through their negative and hateful commentary. It is obviously important to many conservatives with finding fault in others, so to distract the focus away from their own shortcomings while accepting no responsibility for the humanitarian damage to our entire society that they are contributing to through their toxic dialogue day after day.

Journalist *John L. O'Sullivan*, wrote an article in 1839 which, while not using the term "Manifest Destiny", did predict a "divine destiny" for the United States based upon values such as equality, rights of conscience, and personal enfranchisement— "to establish on earth the moral dignity and salvation of man". This destiny was not explicitly territorial, but O'Sullivan predicted that the United States would be one of a "Union of many Republics" sharing those values.

Historian William E. Weeks has noted that three key themes were usually touched upon by advocates of Manifest Destiny:

1. the **virtue** of the American people and their institutions;

2. the **mission** to spread these institutions, thereby redeeming and remaking the world in the image of the U.S.; and

3. the **destiny** under God to accomplish this work.

It is past time to stand up for what our forefathers destined as our unalienable right to live free while demonstrating at all times, greater compassion towards all mankind. I suggest more people try what has always worked for me to maintain forward motion throughout life, when the beliefs and opinions people have been contrary to your own, simply transfer the hate and anger felt towards another person over to disappointment in them, knowing there is nothing that can change who they are and thereby letting you get on with your own life again without the pent-up anxiety towards the way things are that remain out of your control to change!

I hope to use the practical knowledge I've assimilated over the past half century to help provide a more secure and harmonious pathway forward for every man, woman and child to find greater meaning and purpose along their brief journey we all have to enjoy fully here on Earth. Born gifted with the ability to problem solve the most insurmountable challenges I've undertaken throughout my lifetime when doing so my way, gives me greater confidence in finding timely and lasting solutions to try and minimize the untold challenges still ahead for mankind, but only when others take the leap of faith to ask what's still possible and what they can do to become part of the solutions now critical in turning the country back around where the once revered American Way of Life prevails once more. I know President Biden has the moral and ethical competency to act on much needed changes in America, but it requires the American people to now stand unified and denounce the continued dysfunction in Washington, speaking out against any further delays or distractions from lawmakers and enjoin as proud Americans to restore the Republic back to the vision the founders intended our nation to always move ahead towards a more perfect union guided through the interests of the people first!

Young people today are not aware of this but I'm hoping the adults in the room are, the counterproductive, immoral and unethical cycle we've been evolving through in this country over the past half century where the party on the right takes majority control of government only to further their own agenda methodically taking the nation in the wrong direction, then the party on the left when assuming majority power, spends the next 4-8 years restoring some semblance of order to the chaos remaining and placing people's lives on hold, where we take 10 steps back and the 2 steps forward again, is no longer sustainable in America, if we can ever try and evolve into a more perfect union!

Chapter 1

America is in a holding pattern. There is stormy weather in every direction. The turbulence makes it impossible to land and there isn't enough fuel to get above the weather, any suggestions? I know, let's call President Biden out for taking classified documents home or set up committees to investigate the location of Hillary's emails and Hunter Biden's laptop since the public is far more entertained by Republicans distracting people's attention away from the growing challenges still ahead rather than have members of Congress return to the duties each are Constitutionally responsible in performance of the work required by the American people who hired them to represent our interests first! In their defense, lawmakers have not been able to find an equitable balance between the work they are required to complete and political fund raising for future re-election campaigns so maybe it's time for people to accept the fact that partisan interests Congress maintains are more important to members than addressing the perilous challenges still ahead in restoring the democracy or saving mankind from the dangerous effects climate changes has already had on the environment!

If the American still people think that most of their elected officials look at citizens as anything other than 'one vote' for them to gain enough support and enter the highest offices in Washington to then further the self-serving ambitions they have towards greater wealth and power, they are sadly mistaken and reminded after every election cycle how people's errors in judgement continue to take the country in the wrong direction. As the country becomes more divided and insecure with each passing day and people continue to lose trust in one another and those we always thought would provide the security and protections for all Americans whenever our health and wellbeing was threatened as it remains today, begs the question who can we trust going forward to provide us a helping hand whenever we find the need of assistance through no fault of our own?

Have you ever thought what it would be like to go for a job interview with a perspective employer in the private sector and when asked by the hiring committee what makes you more qualified for the position posted over other applicants applying for the same opening? With your response then being, I should be able to meet the job requirements listed but if not, you still can't fire me since the American people determined, from what I told them, that I am the most qualified candidate for the open position and you have no authority to override their decision now! Then you would go on to describe the terms and conditions of your future employment with this 'public service' employer showing that termination is not within their purview to decide, even if found breaking the law at work or negligent in performance of duties required in the job description. In addition, under your own terms and conditions of employment it states you don't have to come into work at any time or attend meetings or work well with others and expect a six-figure salary to be deposited into your bank account on a regular monthly schedule including full health benefits provided and a generous retirement package! Seems like a fantasy job scenario, doesn't it? Well, it's not in Washington because that's the manner in which elected officials see their positions maintained after entering the highest offices in Federal Government under their own terms of employment simply because they say they are and never challenged to the contrary! Today known felons like Richard Santos, who has eluded authorities in this and other countries and shown to have shady ties with Russian Oligarch's while fabricating his character references and can still get a job in Congress simply because he says he can, brings to light the reply spoken time and time again from one of the greatest orators of all time, Americas 44th president, Barack Obama, "really!"

With no guarantees what tomorrow will bring and the country now moving perilously in the wrong direction and further into uncharted territory with no guideposts or safeguards remaining to provide a more secure pathway for the innocent members of society to navigate out of harm's way on their own, demands We the People stand more unified, in solidarity to tell those who still lead with a conscience that the time is now to call out the malevolent bad actors in power and hold them accountable for the crimes against humanity they continue to wage when placing partisan interests ahead of the people's needs during this most critical juncture our nation rests today.

Did you know that the current budget aside from military spending in Washington would cover the costs of creating a more equitable living environment for all Americans so people would begin to feel more content in their day to day lives with their basic needs for food, shelter and health care always being maintained as a human right that we all deserve regardless of the financial circumstances anyone finds themselves in, especially when it's through no fault of their own. By simply streamlining the tax code and reining in obsolete or redundant spending throughout all branches of government and all Americans paying their fair share of taxes back into the system that has provided so many their luxurious lifestyle beyond what most people would expect for themselves, will only then begin to create a more harmonious culture for everyone to live with dignity throughout their lives here on Earth.

The societal attitudes and norms in this country have now migrated to a point where accepting personal responsibility for our own misguided judgments has diminished to a level where it is far easier to just blame someone else for the way things are instead of looking inside one's self to start accepting some responsibility on your own so we as a country can begin repairing the damage already done to America, Planet Earth and people's lives, because it's morally right to do so. We were once a country that led by example through innovation and forward-thinking ideas that would pave a more progressive pathway forward so young people could look upon the role models in their lives, as inspiration to explore their own curiosities into the future, looking back only to learn from the mistakes made in the past! Today America is viewed as a nation lying in wait, unable to move forward into the 21st century now 23 years later where people are told to do no more or less than is necessary in their life to simply try and get by on their own one day at a time. How sad that assessment is of a country once revered around the globe as the most progressive nation on earth, now fallen from grace, free falling further behind other industrialized nations with few opportunities and innovation offered to try and take the lead forward again, especially since those who could change the counterproductive course, we remain on now see little benefit to themselves in doing so.

The previous president never accepted any responsibility for his blatant incompetence and malevolent acts against humanity sending a clear message to the most impressionable members of society showing if you choose not to take any responsibility for your egregious behavior towards others then it's ok to find fault with others and mask your own shortcomings and poor judgement and deflect the truth about the person who you really are. Whatever opinions you may have about President Biden at least he continues to show Americans the moral and ethical competency with which he has to make decisions in the best interest of the people and country first. With a nation now divided and hope towards a brighter future ahead dimming in the minds of the people today, should provide a wakeup call to those who grew up in time now gone by, where pride in America and love of country was ingrained in our human psyche knowing our homeland stood out as the Greatest Nation on Earth for our children to pursue the American Dream in through unlimited joy and happiness along the way, when today seeing that vision of America moving towards a more perfect union, is quickly slipping away.

There was never any ambiguity in the job description of our legislators as stated in the Constitution showing guideposts for members of Congress to adhere by the Rule of Law as it applies to all citizens equally. If they need to be reminded what their sworn duties are to all Americans, simply put, it is to meet the expectations of their constituents who hired them to represent their needs and recognize the Voice of the People first and foremost.

Members of Congress site amendments to the Constitution for reasoning behind the decisions they make when in fact the framers of the Articles of Freedom and Democracy carefully worded every passage contained in those doctrines as guideposts for one standard Rule of Law to be drafted without ambiguity behind the intent as it applies to all citizens equally. The First Amendment is very clear about the right to freedom of speech not being absolute by anyone and subject to limitations such as libel, slander or essentially lying about the character of another individual to further distract attention away from your own shortcomings as we see in the political arena day after day. There is no provision in the Second Amendment that allows military grade weaponry to be in the hands of civilians, period! If there remain any questions as to the founder's original intent behind the carefully worded passages in these and other Amendments to the Constitution then Congress has the power to draft changes that align more closely to societal attitudes today.

We have a climate of uncertainty in America and a greater disregard towards one another's inalienable right to believe and think as they alone have always had the freedom in America to do so, until now! The conservative, right wing faction in Washington continues working 24/7 to agitate and divide the citizens of this great country. They have no solutions to any of the problems we face as a society except to find fault with everyone who expresses views different than theirs. When walking down the halls with news media personnel present, lawmakers throw out words like: more jobs, lower taxes, smaller government, huge deficit, aging out of touch president, privatize entitlements, ship migrant children back home, lower wages, women's rights are for men to decide, citizens have the 2nd Amendment right to bear arms and carry military grade weaponry, slavery had its benefits for some, and on and on and on, noting in the end they are just mere words being espoused with no tangible meaning except to arouse attention in the minds of those whose lives are guided only through sound bites!

Conservatives and obstructionists point their plastic fingers at President Biden and those with differing opinions and ideas contrary to the ones they alone hold, while their silence remains deafening surrounding the overwhelming malevolent and egregious acts driven by the words and actions of the previous president. Do lawmakers really think throwing out talking points on their way to the airport while leaving Washington for yet more personal time off, makes for a convincing argument to most American's people that they have things under control back home? Many living in rural America have been able to function just fine in their day to day lives with a distorted glimpse into the events happening outside the insulated environment they exist in, simply by hearing the sound bites espoused according to the gospel of Fox News commentators and hearing overtones from Pepto Abysmal who even though he remains somewhat out of public view today, continues his toxic rhetoric on how best to Make America Fall Further Into Disgrace, then it already has today!

My generation questioned everything these so-called authoritarian figures in Washington spoke out against, whenever the decisions they alone claimed were done so in the best interests of the country and that we as a subculture known as hippies, needed to now get onboard if we wanted to be recognized as true patriots to the American way of life. So, when America declared war on Vietnam and asked for volunteers to go to this unknown part of the world and eradicate a form of government contrary to ours, young men in my generation started to question what was really going on here asking what this 'shuck n' jive' Washington was selling had to do with us? Young people continued protesting the atrocities of conflict, peacefully marching while declaring to President Nixon that we would rather make love not war thank you your Hineass! Meanwhile in the background while drinking vintage Ripple Wine or Bud Light we were starting to look North into Canada should we ever be called into active duty since it was contrary to our core beliefs being directed to do so! The only barrier we saw should migration over the border then became the last resort for us going forward now, was learning a foreign language and where to place the 'Aaah' in the sentence.

More than ever before it is becoming apparent that America is no longer the glowing star of hope and opportunity it once was, but rather moving in the direction of a third world country, where the rich and powerful dictate what's in their own best interests ahead of the needs of the people and good of the country first. As I continue to show there are timely and lasting solutions to fix most of what remains wrong in America today once members of Congress return to the job responsibilities they have and start to address the backlog of critical issues that have been ignored far too long now, through their needless distractions and delays continuing to take the country in the wrong direction. Unfortunately, though, without leaders ever being challenged for their blatant contempt to abide by the Rule of Law and begin to guide the country under the moral and ethical competency now required more than ever to change the self-destructive course the nation remains on, the American people are left to live their lives one day at a time, doing no more or less than they are required to maintain a semblance of normalcy within the environment we all exist in today.

Some people certainly do not want to hear this but as I see it, the root of most that has gone wrong with America today evolves around responsibility, or better yet people not accepting any responsibility for their own words spoken or actions taken. Yikes, that hurt man! "It's not my fault" is the modern-day response to everything gone bad in someone's life. If you want to see just how endemic the problem has become in America today just watch a few episodes of Judge Judy to see how out of touch people have become with their place in society not accepting any responsibility for their actions towards another person. Just when I thought someone's performance on the daily broadcast was Emmy material, another person will come on the show and take the new leadership position in the blame game saying it's not the pit bulls fault it bit someone but the person moving too quickly around the animal.

There is far more enrichment in life when you become part of the solutions necessary for positive changes to be found in your own lives rather than continuing to be part of the problem by remaining silent in complicity with all that is wrong in America today!

I need to pose this question again because I think it should be on all our minds as we start to navigate the challenges of life before each of us. If you put all your past and present ideals, beliefs and prejudices aside and just ask this one question I am sure most people in this country will come up with the same response:

What have the majority of our elected officials ever done for us or our loved ones to directly improve the quality of life we've experienced during our time so far on planet Earth? The answer will be almost unanimous: little to nothing! Unless you are wealthy or politically connected, you and I only represent to those in power, a means to an end towards fulfilling their own self-serving goals in life, on the backs of every hard-working American in exchange.

Some catastrophic event such as the Covid pandemic that we are still navigating through today may be the only way for more people to put their differences aside and ban together to provide comfort to those most in need. Having experienced and lived through three downturns in our economy and one natural disaster, I have witnessed the capacity in humans to demonstrate compassion for one another especially in a time of need. The uncertain times we as a society find ourselves in today are being overshadowed and almost diminished in plain sight by those responsible for the very challenges, we still face in all our lives now. The evil doers are deflecting the truth about their involvement in critical issues growing more unresolved with each passing day. They have absolutely no solutions to offer other than to do nothing. The message is even more absurd than that as they speak out in public view to just put them back in charge so they can guarantee the status quo mentality remains and assure the wealthy and special interests' supporters that their requests will always be met first. And even more extreme than all this empty rhetoric is that because people are so angry and disillusioned with the current establishment not acting more aggressively to right the wrongs brought on by the previous administration that they feel their only option now is to side with the fringe extremists promising changes that have yet to ever happen even when they hold the majority. These people add laughter to our mundane lives, only thing is that we are laughing at them instead of with them as they choose to live their lives in their own reality while ignoring the pain and suffering, they are causing to so many during their quest for greater fame and power at the expense of bringing the entire country further to its knees.

Did you know that America's first President, George Washington, did not belong to a political party. Most of America's founding fathers were opposed to a two-party system of governance, speaking out to the threats posed to the Republic when one party sought to gain greater power over the other to further their own interests over those of the people and country first. Sadly, the founders were right when we see how fractured our democracy has now become with the radical Republicans always trying to seize greater power from the Democrats only to further their own self-serving needs!

The current party system in America is exactly what the founding fathers abhorred when allowing such a process to be enacted. It breeds self-serving, ego driven motives surrounding one purpose, and that is greed. That a suit with a checkbook could walk outside their office and down the street to "purchase" a favor from someone who was entrusted to represent the people's needs first and foremost, is not only unethical but unlawful under the Rule of Law as its intended to apply equally to all citizens.

How did our government in America become so corrupt? I would like to believe that it all started innocently, where no one was really supposed to get hurt. Where someone or some group had an agenda or set of values, they needed to gain support with. Having the power to "convince" another person to believe in your ideals, constitutes a form of brainwashing. If it is a moral or spiritual belief perhaps it is harmless. If it is a political agenda benefiting a few, it can be the most destructive form of persuasion. Such as the case made by our government leaders justifying most wars, we have entered into over the centuries in Americas past history of decisions gone so immorally wrong.

The time has come and we the people have a process now put in place by our founding fathers that demands change if our "Form of Government ever becomes destructive of these ends".

We hold these truths to be self-evident, that all men are created equal, that they are endowed by their Creator with certain unalienable Rights, that among these are Life, Liberty and the Pursuit of Happiness.—That to secure these rights,

Governments are instituted among citizens, deriving their just powers from the consent of the governed, -- **That whenever any Form of Government becomes destructive of these ends, it is the Right of the People to alter or to abolish it, and to institute new Government, laying its foundation on such principles and organizing its powers in such form, as to them shall seem most likely to affect their Safety and Happiness. The Declaration of Independence signed into law July 4, 1776.**

For too many years our elected officials have spent recklessly, made self-serving decisions not in our best interest and the most heinous act of all, wasted our precious time on this earth suppressing our ability to pursue the 'American Dream' in health, wealth and happiness while being able to practice goodwill towards our fellow man.

When in the Course of human events, it becomes necessary for one people to dissolve the political bands which have connected them with another, and to assume among the powers of the earth, the separate and equal station to which the Laws of Nature and of Nature's God entitle them, a decent respect to the opinions of mankind requires that they should declare the causes which impel them to the separation.

The clock is ticking faster for some, so let's stop debating nonissues and begin instituting a system of honor and privilege for anyone working in public service with respect for the position they hold to do what is right for America and the future of humanity simply because they should and can deliver on the promises made to the American people! There is nothing to stop us from demanding change to our continued dysfunctional form of government in America today with this being the only way we will ever be able to assure our children they will be free and secure to follow their ambitions fully knowing the pathway forward in pursuit of the American Dream will be discovered through untold joy and happiness along the way!

Chapter 2

The 1st amendment of the US Constitution defines the intent of the law as drafted by our forefathers:

Freedom of speech is the freedom to speak without *censorship* and/or *limitation*. The synonymous term **freedom of expression** is sometimes used to indicate not only freedom of verbal speech but any act of seeking, receiving and imparting information or ideas, regardless of the medium used. In practice, the right to freedom of speech is not absolute in any country and the right is commonly subject to limitations, such as on "*hate speech*".

The right to freedom of speech is recognized as a human right under Article 19 of the Universal Declaration of Human Rights and recognized in international human rights law in the International Covenant on Civil and Political Rights (ICCPR). The ICCPR recognizes the right to freedom of speech as "the right to hold opinions without interference. Everyone shall have the right to freedom of expression".[1][2] Furthermore freedom of speech is recognized in European, inter-American and African regional human rights law. It is different from and not to be confused with the concept of freedom of thought. The freedom of speech can be found in early human rights documents, such as *Declaration of the Rights of Man and of the Citizen (1789)*, a key document of the French Revolution.[4] The Declaration provides for freedom of expression in Article 11, which states that: "The free communication of ideas and opinions is one of the most precious of the rights of man. Every citizen may, accordingly, speak, write, and print with freedom, but shall be responsible for such abuses of this freedom as shall be defined by law." [5]

Every citizen may accordingly speak, write and print with freedom, **but shall be equally responsible for such abuses of this freedom as shall be defined by law.** When was this interpreted to mean every citizen has the right to speak freely even if someone else is harmed as a result of your slanderous contempt against another person's character? The majority of Americans are becoming defensive and distrustful of their civic leaders as people have now lost trust in their ability to represent, all citizens honestly and with any sense of integrity. People look upon these 'leaders' who we've always trusted with our lives and livelihood, essentially ignore those voices of citizens who gave them their jobs in the first place. These racist, greedy, self-serving bad actors are preaching to a small congregation of their followers though. The missed message continues to be overlooked by lawmakers today, knowing the time it takes to defend your malevolent actions could be used to remedy most of what remains wrong in America without any further delays! Citizens are becoming disenchanted with the finger pointing by members of Congress while President Biden continues to try and bring the nation back from the brink of collapse, remaining once again after the majority on the right took control of government to carry out their evil self-serving deeds. Once more all Americans were left in 'shock and awe' to provide their own means to and end and try and exist on our own, one day at a time.

It should never have become acceptable practice to disparage someone's character in the public sector under the guise that words being spoken are done so in a politically acceptable atmosphere regardless how someone perceives the real intent in which the dialogue is presented by the speaker. If the act is intentional and without merit or facts to support the narrative then those committing the malicious verbal assault against another individual, should then be criminally charged in a civil court and have to pay monetary restitution to the harmed party. Just as in the private sector if someone's livelihood is diminished due to a deliberate and malicious character assassination, the perpetrators can be sued in a court of law. There is currently no civil punishment for verbalizing, publishing or inciting others to defame a public figure with deliberate and malicious intent in causing harm to that person. Especially if you speak out against our elected officials to try and tarnish their reputation in front of all Americans when there are no facts to support the allegations or your perceived justification to do so. And when it is done with malice of forethought for personal gain the act should be one of tyranny and punishable by a prison sentence, so help you God! Only when there are severe consequences for those malicious attacks against another person's character in the public sector as in the private sector, will the evil doers think twice about committing such heinous acts like that ever again.

Doesn't anyone else see the fundamental injustice by some, with their continued abuse of this and other laws? If you want to change the First Amendment so that the law allows this egregious practice to remain then so be it, but the more this injustice continues to proliferate throughout society with no consequences for such deliberate acts of injustice, then it will soon become the accepted practice and just further the 'blame game' to a point of absurdity. I just hope we can someday clone the good actors like Judge Judy because I fear the backlog of cases is about to become too overwhelming for one judge to handle on their own much longer! It also sets the stage for a society being transformed into one without the intellect or character this country was designed where people could once more be able to differentiate between a lie and the truth enshrined within the tried-and-true principles ingrained in each of our human psyches from birth.

Any public figure on record stating their opposing views and then later deceiving the public with contradictory statements being made should be held to their original talking points on record as they can be viewed in plain sight for everyone to witness. Every one of the Republicans and conservative politicians currently in office fought against the enactment of the relief/stimulus package that President Biden put into place without their support after Covid disrupted people's lives and livelihoods beyond remediation and through no fault of our own. But when more people finally began to emerge from solitary confinement through the essential aid being provided from the financial subsidies they received thanks to the president and most Democrats in Congress, Republicans wasted no time spinning the truth once more and taking credit for those in their districts who were starting to get their lives moving more securely ahead, with not one of them voting to help the American people during such a dire time of need that most found themselves in, once again, through no fault of their own!

Leo W. Gerard President of the United Steelworkers International
Posted: December 22, 2008 04:36 PM

A week earlier, 31 GOP Senators, mostly from Southern states, voted to avert their eyes and allow American auto companies to die. They opposed $14 billion in federal loans for GM and Chrysler, revealing that their loyalty lies not with America, not even with their own states, but with South Korea and Germany and Japan.

They are Toyota Republicans.

Toyota has non-union manufacturing plants in Alabama, Kentucky, Mississippi and Texas - states whose senators led the GOP quest to slay the Big Three American auto manufacturers - Richard Shelby, RAla.; Mitch McConnell, R-Ky, and John Cornyn, R-Tx. Here's the Republican from Mississippi, Sen. Thad Cochran, explaining why he'd vote against the loans, "Things have changed. It's not just the Big Three anymore," he said, pointing out that Nissan and Toyota employ more Mississippians than General Motors, Ford and Chrysler. But, he said, the foreign companies would not share "in the benefits of that automobile bailout program."

No. But Mississippi did give Nissan and Toyota more than $650 million to entice them to locate in the state. GM, Ford and Chrysler didn't share in those benefits, Sen. Cochran. The Toyota Republicans are all for helping the rich with tax breaks and shelters, and they're all for aiding foreign auto manufacturers with billions worth of tax forgiveness and government-paid infrastructure improvements.

One of these Toyota Republicans even had the nerve to go to a United Autoworkers rally to take credit for the bailout of the Big Three and congratulate the workers for sticking it out until the automakers got back on their feet after the subsidy from the government. Even after he voted to let the US automakers go out of business so the foreign automakers could compete more freely in America! I am not making this stuff up, it is all documented on Wiki or somewhere else, believe me or better yet, look it up for yourself.

Chapter 3

Did you know there are practical and lasting solutions to find that will begin to fix most of what remains wrong in America today, while most people live through such uncertain times ahead when the untold challenges still go unanswered around health care for all, gun violence, cost of living, immigration, division and distrust between one another, civil unrest, elections and most importantly climate change, which must be addressed now by those we elected to represent the people's needs and interests first.

So, let's see what can be done today knowing the alternative for people to remain silent any longer, is no longer conducive to finding answers that will begin to ensure hope in people's minds again that a brighter future still lies ahead for them and generations to follow. As I have mentioned before once the core cause behind the rogue dysfunction in Washington is finally revealed and remedied through the nonpartisan action this president can sign into practice now, will then bring into greater focus how human needs and interests must be addressed today. While the untold challenges still lie ahead and without remediating the damage already caused to the country, the planet and people's lives today, leaves little hope in our minds that positive changes can still transpire in time before the next setback we all face takes us further in the wrong direction with little relief in sight again!

So, let's see what's possible once members of Congress are required to uphold the job responsibilities they now have described in the Constitution and return to the work of the people first without further delays:

1. Excessive student debt for most young people first entering the job market outside technical or professional fields where higher education credentials are required, will become a thing of the past. With incentives returning that reward companies providing on-site training for potential job candidates, and applicants being paid a living wage to see if they can meet and hopefully exceed the requirements needed to perform the work standards

described, will expedite the hiring process and allow young people to begin a more productive career track early in life without going into endless debt to begin doing so. Maybe those entering the workplace environment for the first time will be required to hold an Associate Degree so they can have general background knowledge in the field they may be interested in pursuing later on. Even in the professional fields of employment there is a reason that medical and legal fields are listed as 'practices' because it's the only way someone entering those professions will ever gain the expertise and competency in performance of the job, they hold that can't be conveyed in books or lectures but only by practicing in real time whatever their specialty entails. Unfortunately, in those fields of expertise, people are the test subjects in question for Doctors and Lawyers to become better at the performance of the work they are responsible for!

I remember shortly after graduating from Community College with an Associate's Degree in Business Administration, I applied for a position as a computer operator on mainframe computers that was a new field of expertise few people had any prior experience with. The company offered me a living wage at the time to train me in house on what the duties would be to act as an interface between customers running computer software jobs on the mainframe computers that usually filled rooms the size of football fields embossed with the name IBM on the hardware devices. I learned a lot from that job, finding out at someone else's expense, what career track I'd eventually like to pursue long term. I decided to start my own business two years later gaining confidence in my ability to do so with the practical experience I'd assimilated while working with mainframe computers alongside the basic knowledge acquired in the academic environment which was only general in nature but an academic requirement at the time to get my degree.

2. Future Federal Elections will be held electronically, where voters lives will no longer be disrupted in their efforts to try and reach polling locations or standing in long lines remaining uncertain whether their personal choices in candidates will then be officially recorded, since future candidates running for the highest offices in the country will no longer be considered on party line votes alone but must show prior job qualifications in order to be considered for such high-level positions with the Federal Government in the future. Most importantly, we will never again allow white collar conservatives to hold the country hostage while pointing their plastic fingers at us and make false unsubstantiated claims in future elections, that they lost because the system is rigged, when in fact it's because they have

always been identified throughout their empty lives as mentally deficient losers before it was made public for the whole world to see who they really are now. This is the only way gross incompetence and corruption will no longer breach the code of trust and honor once maintained throughout our branches of government where members of Congress and the President swore an oath in their adherence to the stated code of conduct while in office without deviation from performance of the duties listed in the Constitution.

3. Mass shootings and gun violence can be minimized when the wording in Second Amendment to the Constitution is more clearly aligned to reflect the changing times and societal attitudes our country evolves through, stating clearly that 'civilians' have no legal right to keep and bear 'military grade weaponry' for self-defense purposes. Period!

4. These and all other challenges before the country today can be permanently changed with safeguards put in place to assure future generations, we will never allow such egregious acts against humanity to ever be reenacted again! The American people have to come together again, united under one nation, one voice to end the needless delays and distractions by members of Congress who continue wasting time we no longer have and

begin addressing the critical issues holding the nation hostage from ever moving ahead again until the growing challenges we face today are finally resolved. The practical solutions I've already sent to President Biden's attention will start the process immediately with every member of Congress getting back to the job responsibilities they have and complete the work Americans hired them to perform for the good of the country, while protecting and serving the needs of the people foremost! While we are waiting for that much needed change in Congress to fully transpire and showing the American people beyond just words spoken and promises being made, that their future and that of mankind's should now remain the primary focus in Washington with human needs replacing partisan interests from this day forward! Starting with a mandated 4-day, 32-hour work week with everyone being paid a living wage equivalent to their full-time salary agreement. Then on your next paid work day off, people should be required give back to their community volunteering to provide a helping hand to those in need or begin to strengthen your own mental health requirements by attending a free concert in the park complements of the Federal Government. Popular bands will perform concerts all over the country and bring people together of all ages through the mental health initiative called 'MUSIC SETS US FREE AGAIN.' Then wouldn't it be nice when your friends ask if you're going down to the park later to hear Bruce Springsteen or Mumford and Sons perform and you answer them, "I always abide by the law, so of course I'll be there!"

5. Define The Will of the People as 51% of the voting population in America. Then when the question in Washington is asked of voters whether Universal Healthcare should be provided at no cost to all Americans and the electronic polling results returns a minimum of 51% in favor of adopting the proposal, then it will be up to Congress to find the most cost effective and expeditious manner in which to send the bill over to the president for his signature into law. If Congress needs additional time to increase the budget or ways to pay for the proposal still being legislated then they have the responsibility to keep the American people apprised of the progress being made in chambers so citizens can plan around medical issues arising before the bill is actually signed into law. Then as we start to watch news reporting segments throughout the day now presented in a more positive atmosphere and highlighting the progressive transformation already taking place throughout the country and in people's lives because the work that's finally begun to return America to The Greatest Nation on

Earth again, will start to overshadow how much we still need to do. If lawmakers don't share the majority of the people's wishes for much needed changes in our homeland, then they can do what workers do in the private sector by keeping your thoughts, ideas, political beliefs and opinions to yourself while in the workplace environment where the people expect you to perform the duties required since you're well compensated to do no less, Marjorie Taylor Greene! No single lawmaker will ever again be able to vote in opposition or delay legislation being debated on the floor, when a minimum of 51% of the voting public and 51% of their constituents support passage of the measures into law sooner than later.

The possibilities remain limitless throughout people's lives again when our leaders return to the job, they swore to perform in the interests of the people first and decide on matters crucial in maintaining the founder's design for our Republic to be guided through the voice of the people first and foremost.

As I stated before, it is a known fact when countries focus on the health, security and wellbeing of its citizens first then it's proven for those nations to have the most amicable coexistence among people in their communities because the relationship between one another shows we become more content in our own lives when the basic needs each of us has are maintained to provide everyone with a greater sense of dignity along the way. Let's try and return to that model originally conceived for America to evolve into a more perfect union through the tests of time, where generations to follow can find greater meaning and purpose during the journey they have yet to take while in pursuit of the American Dream found through greater joy and happiness along the way.

Time is running out to try and return America to a semblance of its former glory, away from the most insecure, divided and dangerous position it lies in today, when renewing our pledge of allegiance to the flag and country that has always been embraced through the sacrifices made by those who fought with their lives to preserve the image of loyalty to the American Way of Life found when we are united in preserving what has always made us stand out as The Greatest Nation on Earth! The divine right we are granted to remain free, proclaiming the moral imperative we all have before us to choose our own destiny during the brief passage here on Earth, must never be diminished by those who only exist for themselves, taking from others what is not theirs to hold. There remains no ambiguity to the intent in which the founders drafted the carefully worded passages in the Articles of Freedom and Democracy signed in perpetuity inclusive to the rule of law all citizens must abide by when:

WE HOLD THESE TRUTHS TO BE SELF-EVIDENT THAT ALL PEOPLE ARE CREATED EQUAL, THAT THEY ARE ENDOWED BY THEIR CREATORS WITH CERTAIN INALIENABLE RIGHTS, AMONG THESE ARE LIFE, LIBERTY AND THE PURSUIT OF HAPPINESS THROUGHOUT THIS LIFETIME HERE ON EARTH!

The time is now to honor the founders signing of the Declaration of Independence July 4, 1776 incorporating the words written into the Rule of Law as it applies to all citizens equally today, holding these truths to be self-evident, that America will never become the oppressive regime that We the People separated from over two and a half centuries ago in Great Britain. With no guardrails left in place for government in America to function as it was once chartered where the foundational pillars this great nation was conceived within are now dismantled beyond repair, calls on all Americans to stand in solidarity under one voice that speaks the truth our founders declared: WHENEVER ANY FORM OF GOVERNMENT IN AMERICA BECOMES DESTRUCTIVE OF THESE ENDS, IT IS THE INALIENABLE RIGHT OF THE PEOPLE TO ALTER OR ABOLISH IT, AND TO INSTITUTE NEW GOVERNMENT, LAYING ITS FOUNDATION ON SUCH PRINCIPLES AND ORGANIZING ITS POWERS IN SUCH A FORM AS TO THEM SEEM MOST TO EFFECT THEIR SAFETY AND HAPPINESS. These are not just words written in annals of our nation's history now filed deep into the National Archives, but guideposts for people to honor the founder's intent when creating this Republic for the people to direct, guaranteeing our protection and interests will always be served unconditionally through the tests of time as our nation continues to evolve into a more perfect union!

That is why I've provided President Biden a way to get our great nation moving forward again once he honors the commitment made to the American people in the last election that begins rebuilding our now fractured democracy with all members of Congress returning to the duties, they swore an oath to uphold while in office, that makes them accountable in representing the interests of their constituents and serving the needs of the American people foremost. Slow incremental changes suggested to begin fixing the almost insurmountable challenges still ahead in most people's lives today alongside all the needless delays and distractions coming from members of Congress, will remain a futile attempt to try and change the country's course in time with climate change already dangerously altering the environment that all life must be sustained in as long as possible. This is another reason I've tried to show President Biden the urgency with which he must act sooner than later to implement the nonpartisan procedural changes suggested so every member of Congress must immediately return to the job requirements they have shown in the Constitution, assembling in a more collaborative work place environment where critical issues before the nation today are addressed without further delays or distractions.

The first thing the American people have to do is recognize that the founding fathers fought with their lives to ensure every man, woman and child had unalienable rights to live free, prosper and pursue happiness in a democratic society. These rights have now been taken away from the majority of law-abiding American citizens. Politicians have sold the American people out to special interests. Greed drives those in power with no regard or compassion for our human rights. The American people remain the decision makers on living wages, job creation, universal health care and equal rights for everyone, while the government acts to find the most fiscally responsible way to enact laws, then administer the changes while providing the oversight required to maintain a balance of order under one standard Rule of Law as it applies to all citizens.

Once the country gets back on track again in a more secure and cohesive environment for people to then decide for themselves their own future plans ahead, leaders in Washington need to set up committees to discuss matters that have always contradicted our core beliefs ingrained in our human psyche when knowing between right and wrong, good and bad behavior now brought out by those we've always entrusted with our lives to protect each of us from harm's way in a time of need that we all live through today, still seeing now relief in sight!

- Unless a president can convince the American people that planned military conflicts outside our country are essential to enter into for our own safety here at home, then we need to think about redirecting those funds to protect our own borders instead. Maybe we could beef up the satellite defense system in this country in the event other countries pose a threat by attacking us on American soil, North Korea. We do need to rotate staff in those bunkers though so they don't become tired of waiting to push the button while falling asleep and accidentally laying their heads down on the button. Those 'domes' as seen in the movies seem like a good idea also. The money we save by not having our military personnel deployed to other countries that we have no business being in without some support from our allies, could instead be used to strengthen and secure our borders here at home. If other countries want to contract out the security manpower we have from US based firms that specialize in that, then I'm sure there are a lot of idle mercenaries looking for extra work, without our country always supplying American troops and munitions to further those nations causes while our own hidden agenda needs more oversight to determine if it's worth the cost in human lives to engage in conflicts, we have no business entering into in the first place.

- We have to stop giving money to other countries for the sole purpose of buying their allegiance. If it is for humanitarian reasons that

Americans contribute taxpayer dollars to other governments, the case must be made that it will be used only for the intended cause and be a loan whenever possible. I was always suspicious when someone had to pay for friendship or buy allegiance from someone else, when their association could be built on the premise of an equal partnership endeavor, such as the case with most humanitarian outreach goals.

- The single largest outlay of taxpayer dollars next to military spending is waste. Waste due to fraud, waste due to lack of oversight and waste due to lack of enforcement of the tax code and mismanagement of social programs designed to assist the disadvantaged population. The Bush II administration and Trump Period Debacle not only turned a blind eye to any oversight in banking and Wall Street but it encouraged creative instruments of investment to help its wealthy contributors get even wealthier at the expense of millions of hard-working Americans losing their livelihoods. We could immediately put thousands of people to work on oversight committees. Private sector workers could then monitor Medicare claims, Senator Rick Scott from Florida, that are batch processed to track fraudulent billing practices from health practitioners. How many tongue depressors does anyone physician really need? Teams of workers could audit wealthy citizen's tax returns for fraudulent deductions or exemptions. These citizen oversight commissions could not only pay for themselves by identifying fraudulent claims made but also providing backup information to the agencies cracking down on the repeat offenders and bringing criminal investigations into the forefront to try and discourage others from not paying their fair share of taxes. Oversight commission staff would essentially be paid to 'rat out' those trying to cheat the government and maybe be given bonuses for bringing to justice, the repeat offenders who continually act outside the rule of law as it was designed to apply equally to all citizens. Those sitting on citizen's oversight committees would make sure funds are being disbursed as intended through Medicare, Medicaid and Social Security. The current system of contracting out to private companies, to enforce the provisions regulating the claims process within our entitlement programs, is not working as well as it could. Without additional incentives offered to these private firms to crack down further on fraud and waste within our entitlement programs, abuses will continue within our current systems in place.

- The Justice System is another area that needs to be changed. Special interests, specifically attorneys and judges have manipulated the intent of the laws to suit their own political agenda, like decisions made to allow governors how best to address immigration reform by busing illegals coming over their borders who are seeking refuge from an oppressive regime in their homelands, to unfamiliar locations they are then left to navigate ahead on their own. We are practically inviting criminals to commit crimes because they know through due process, they will be given legal defense with certain rights to lessen or even overthrow their convictions. The only way we are going to deter criminals is hold them accountable for their crimes, especially those of sound mind and who cause intentional harm to another living being. If someone physically causes severe harm to another person more than once then they need to be incarcerated for the duration of their lives without any chance for parole. The people need to vote on changes to laws validated by the Supreme Court if their rulings bring into question some contradiction with the core personal beliefs of most citizens have in this country. The recent ruling by the Supreme Court overturning Roe v Wade is such an abhorrent act against humanity stating outright that the government is the final decision maker in a woman's personal health decisions, knowing what's in her own best interests better than she does herself is immoral and should not stand! Nine appointed individuals should never be allowed to change laws such as Roe v Wade or their ruling on Citizens United, identifying corporations as people too! Really!

- Immigration reform has become such moral imperative and complicated issue to deal with, no one really wants to take an aggressive stance with solving the problem. Racial profiling as the State of

Arizona led the movement in past Republican lead administrations is certainly not the answer when identifying whether someone has a right to be in this country or not. 'Papers Please' is such an abhorrent abuse of the law that the governor should have been recalled after her support of such an attack of everyone's civil liberties in this country. I know personally I will never step foot in that state again. Maybe we should start to address the problem by closing the borders completely, slowing the migrant influx into our country until we get more of our current citizens employed again and our economy turned around. Why compound the problem with greater competition for jobs, resources and social programs within our own country. The only way we are ever going to determine if someone really wants to work and provide for themselves and their family and not rely on subsidies is to provide opportunities to all citizens able and willing to work. The only way we can do that is to become a self-sufficient country again taking pride in 'Made in America.' If we can start to live within our means and be paid a living wage then we can start to work for less and bring manufacturing jobs back into this country. Many immigrants coming to America are hardworking individuals willing to work for less and perform jobs others would rather not do. There is no reason we cannot grant citizenship to those members of our society willing to make a positive contribution and bring jobs back to America so we are not so dependent on foreign goods. Of course, if opportunities are given but not taken because some able-bodied citizens will never be motivated to make a positive contribution to society, then we should probably take away their safety net so they understand the need to be a part of the solution as opposed to always just contributing the problem.

There are real solutions to be found that permanently fix most of what remains wrong in people's lives but only when we as a society alongside elected officials begin thinking beyond the status quo mentality that continues to leave the country and people's lives in stasis today. With no direction or guidance coming out of Washington to show the American people that there are tangible advancements being made to move the nation forward into the 21st century, now 23 years later, only continues to provide little hope in people's minds that their own lives will ever return to a semblance of normalcy again.

Let's join together again and return the decision making back to the people who know better than anyone what each of us needs and desires in our own lives yet to be lived fully, with the interests we as human beings still have, to enjoin under one nation again and come together as true patriots to the once enamored way of life only found here in The Greatest Nation on Earth once more! Life is short, there are no guarantees what tomorrow will bring so remember humans are all on planet earth to live each and every day to the fullest, through greater happiness and joy along the way! We all arrived here in this realm of existence with a one-way ticket and once we step on the Dearly Departed Bus out of the town, will not be returning here on planet earth in our current form anytime soon!

Chapter 4

So how do we get started and energize the good citizens of this great nation to finally stand up for those inalienable rights granted to *all* Americans as human beings at birth and from our founding fathers who designed this Republic through the voice and demands of, We the People first and foremost.

First and as, I've discussed previously, it's past time to move the Federal Elections process into the 21st century so everyone can cast their votes for the candidate's they choose, via a text or when a unique passcode is sent to you based on your personal voting criteria on file at the local county registrar's office, then ballots can be sent over to your computer to complete and returned that day. Also, with the candidate's now running for the highest offices in the land requiring their prior work history to show they are qualified to hold such important elected positions with the Federal Government, there will no longer be the backlash and needless waste of resources by those contesting the results of the final count, based on party affiliation alone.

It should be compulsory that all legal citizens upon turning 18 years of age register to vote in this country. Then when a general election is held or call to vote on an initiative by citizens, 51% of the registered voters need to be determined to elect or re-elect a president or when adopting new laws. With compulsory voting requirements enacted, failure to record the required percentage of votes for a new or reelected president or enactment of new laws will easily be determined as null and void during that election or a call-for-vote request. If none of the candidates running for president for the first time, receive the required 51% of the popular votes to be elected, then a secondary list of candidates need to be available for a timely, second attempt to vote a president into office. If the president is up for re-election and doesn't receive 51% of the votes needed to stay in office for a second term and neither do the candidates running against the president, then perhaps a secondary list of candidates can quickly be identified and voted on to try and determine a winner with 51% of the popular votes. This is a very simplified idea to try and at least get people thinking and government officials currently involved in our election process, to present alternative ways of electing our president and allowing laws to be enacted. The new voting laws would be absent the current partisan influence that adversely affects the outcomes of the election process in place today.

Compulsory voting

One of the strongest factors affecting voter turnout is whether voting is compulsory. In Australia, voter registration and attendance at a polling booth have been mandatory since the 1920s. These rules are strictly enforced, and the country has one of the world's highest voter turnouts. Several other countries have similar laws, generally with somewhat reduced levels of enforcement. If a Bolivian voter fails to participate in an election, the citizen may be denied withdrawal of their salary from the bank for three months. In Mexico and Brazil, existing sanctions for non-voting are minimal or are rarely enforced. When enforced, compulsion has a dramatic effect on turnout.

With intentional gerrymandering of districts by Republicans here in America today, brings to the forefront, corrupted voting practices at the polls by conservatives while the losers in that party refuse to accept their defeat, guaranteeing that the voting public has all but lost their protections given to everyone equally under the Constitution of The United States of America. With politics sidelined from our rule of governance in this country, the risk of rigging the system in favor of one candidate over another is greatly reduced, if not completely eliminated. This would then force scam artists to come up with a new and improved way to try and pull the wool over the eyes of the voters, meanwhile it's back to business in a more pro-active, organized and less dysfunctional form of government that we maintain today.

Chapter 5

Is change still possible or is it time to admit to ourselves the foundational pillars this Republic, as they were always envisioned to support a more progressive and unified direction for the American people to decide how the nation will evolve through the changing times into a more perfect union, have now crumbled beyond repair, where America will soon be recognized around the globe, as a Failed Experiment in Democracy?

I still believe today as I always have, that failure is never an option as long as we can gain the strength needed to overcome adversity and navigate around the challenges people now face in their own lives knowing positive change once sought out, can bring about new and exciting avenues forward during the brief passage we all have to live life fully here on earth. That is why I've tried to convey the message to President Biden that failure is not an option for the American people to ever accept, if he and members of Congress are to honor the commitment, they've always made in protecting and serving the needs of the American people first and foremost, through the tests of time. The country now lays in wait before any positive changes will ever come about again and the core cause behind the counter productive dysfunction in Washington is finally addressed.

So how can we get started changing the needless division and distrust we have in one another when people are told to take political sides as a way to have perfect strangers then manage your life their way, leaving most Americans today waiting in hopeful anticipation that their personal lives will return to normal again when it's already determined to get far worse as mankind will no longer be able to remediate the damage we've already done to the planet and Mother Earth then steps in to determine humanity's fate going forward! I now urge parents specially to start thinking forward on behalf of your children's fate and that of generations to follow when we come together as one to:

1. Believe in the ability we all have to overcome adversity in our own lives when more people come together, united as one, to become part of the solutions essential now more than ever, to begin an address the untold challenges still ahead, when working together alongside those who have been given the absolute authority to decide on matters in the best interests of the people and country first.

2. Believing that the 'Will of the People' is a fundamental human right promised to everyone in America wishing to live free through compassion and goodwill towards all mankind.

3. Restore the self-confidence in yourself to find some meaning and purpose through the endeavors you pursue then doing so finding greater joy and happiness along the way.

4. Even if you haven't the ambition or drive to try and redirect your moral compass that guides each of us to become more compassionate towards one another, then why not secure the resources you already have to provide a more sustainable pathway forward for those who enter this realm of existence we're in now who may be seeking a helping hand after we've departed. The humanist actions demonstrated by the founder of Patagonia who recently allocated the future profits of the company he created, over to groups trying to sustain all life on the planet through the continued efforts shown in slowing global warming and begin managing the damage already caused to the environment that all living creatures must try and exist throughout as long as possible, is truly admirable!

5. Realize that change is always a slow process even under the best of conditions but with so many uncertainties facing mankind today and the challenges mounting to try and manage them

before the next interruption in all our lives can appear at any time as COVID did, leaves little time to try and debate longer what must be done now to start and address the critical issues before we move further into uncharted territory with no contingency plans on how to safely navigate the perils that still lie ahead. Time has truly run out to debate 'what if' but it is now ever more critical for the future of humanity to discuss the most effective and timely way to move past the errors in judgement we've all made in the past now placing the country, the planet and people's lives in harm's way, with no safeguards remaining to provide us greater protection when we will need it the most!

6. What if you could change the current course your life remains on today where you'd wake up each work day going into where the job was actually stimulating and more challenging when asked to use your creative ability, being trained and paid to think outside the box and come up with new and exciting ways that will move the country and people's lives into the 21st century and beyond because you participated in transforming America back to a leader in innovation once more! I started my own company during the dot com era when Silicon Valley was such a vibrant place to work in, where the innovative, forward thinking spirit people had, provided a beacon of light in most people's mind that the future now held so much promise in our lives, glowing ever so brightly with each passing day. Back then we weren't distracted

by what wasn't being accomplished but how much more promise there was in our own the future and for the country overall when we could work together focusing on the common good in people while initially showing respect in one another's right to express their own ideas and opinions as long as they didn't try and intimidate us into thinking ours were outside mainstream ideals and needed to align more closely to theirs going forward. There are ways to change the cultural norms and societal attitudes back to a place where people are no longer misguided in the belief that we must choose political sides over respect for the right everyone has to hold differing opinions and beliefs as long as they don't try and indoctrinate others, against their wishes, to accept a way of thinking contrary to their own.

7. People must begin to accept responsibility for your own actions whatever the repercussions may be when admitting the errors in judgement you've had that hopefully you'll learn from those mistakes made so not to repeat them again. Many people go through life thinking that when things go wrong and they are personally harmed in any way, it always has to be someone else's fault. I encourage everyone to reflect on the words of one of the greatest Arbiters of all times telling litigants presenting their case before her on national tv, "if you tell the truth, you don't need to have a good memory," when presenting a more fact-based defense to convince others that the claim being

made against you with your actions causing harm to someone else, really wasn't your fault.

8. Most importantly speak out against those whose narrative contradicts our ingrained beliefs about right and wrong, good and bad behavior, otherwise your continued silence only incentivizes those who act without a moral conscience to continue their malevolent acts against others and deflect the truth away from the fact that they are only looking out for themselves.

9. The most important thing people need to realize now that time is no longer on humanity's side to delay any longer the need for permanent fixes to most of what remains wrong in America today so we can be better prepared for the greatest threat to mankind now on the horizon through climate change. Incremental fixes to a now broken and dysfunctional form of government in America will remain an exercise in futility to try and restore our homeland back to a nation we can all take pride in calling The Greatest Nation on Earth once more.

Chapter 6

I grew up in a generation where a number of our elected officials became role models for us to mentor in our own lives because they exhibited the moral and ethical character we learned to expect from leaders in Washington, showing their dedication to the performance of the work they were responsible for carrying out and honoring the positions they were elected to hold in trust, with the interests of the American people being maintained unconditionally throughout their tenure in public office. This would then provide needed guide posts for more people to try and live their own lives more ingenuous towards others, doing so with the moral and ethical conscience our elected officials in Washington were always expected to do in support of the words and actions they lead the nation through example while enshrined in the rich way of life once synonymous with Life in America.

This brought to mind the admiration shown by young and older people alike when John F. Kennedy, the youngest president ever elected into the highest office in the land, spoke in his Inaugural Address through the memorable injunction: Ask not what your country can do for you ask what you can do for your country."

These words have never provided more stimulus today for We the People united as 'one' and standing in solidarity asking one another, what all Americans must now do to resurrect our fractured and divided Republic since those responsible for maintaining the image this great nation was once revered around the globe, have now knowingly let it fall from grace beyond their repair alone! This now leaves the choice up to all citizens whether remaining silent any longer can change the destructive course America remains on today before the next alteration in our lives derails further plans to try and do so in time!

Role Models have always set examples for the way we should pattern our own lives yet to be lived fully, always doing so in unison with the core beliefs that are ingrained in the human psyche from birth, instinctively knowing right from wrong, good and bad behavior when the words and actions shown by others contradict those humanistic ideals known to guide societies in a more harmonious and compassionate direction through the tests of time. It's past time to return to that model America was always envisioned to evolve into a more perfect union, lead through the voices of the people speaking out whenever those we always entrusted to protect and serve our citizens needs first, have decided to breach the terms and conditions of the contract they swore to uphold for God and country while disregarding the Constitutional duties they have to perform for the people and country unconditionally.

I had the unique opportunity when starting my own business to be personally mentored by one of the most respected entrepreneurs and humanist leaders in modern day times, where David Packard was a role model of mine who guided me to follow the aspirations, I set out to explore by taking greater risks along the way as a means to ultimately problem solve the challenges ahead more effectively. Sitting in his office at Hewlett Packard in Palo Alto, California, he told me to think beyond mainstream beliefs and ideals to come up with more innovative and practical methods to move forward again, knowing mistakes will be made along the way but learning from those errors in judgement remained the only way to test the full potential people have to try and succeed in the end, aspiring always to be the best we can be.

I went on to run a successful enterprise of my own for a quarter century while showing the respect and gratitude towards the customers and people working alongside me that seemed ingrained throughout the workplace ethic at Hewlett Packard Company used as my model and giving me greater self-confidence to overcome the challenges I faced as a sole proprietor while continuing to grow the business beyond all expectations!

That is why I've tried to show ways for this president to get the country moving ahead again when taking greater risks in the decisions he makes, beyond the status quo mentality that continues to lead the nation and people's lives further in the wrong direction while taking the entire country further into dangerous uncharted territory with no safety nets in place to prepare people for the worst yet to come in climate change!

So, what do you say knowing there is everything to gain and so much more to lose when We the People are unable to enjoin as one voice and speak out indivisible through our human desire to change the self-destructive course mankind remains on in America today, doing so as Role Models for young people to now reflect on their own lives going forward in a way, they will be inspired do the same for generations to follow!

LET'S GET STARTED

Chapter 7

The first thing, 'We the People' need to do once all our voices are heard again and inclusive in the decisions being made by leaders throughout Washington around the health, security and wellbeing of all citizens first alongside their undivided attention being laser focused on ways to get the country moving ahead by addressing most of what remains wrong in America today with permanent solutions found around the critical issues that can no longer be fixed incrementally!

Then and only then will we be able to look into the eyes of a child once more and assure them the pathway ahead for generations to follow will never again be as insecure as it exists in today, with such uncertain times ahead that we will no longer ignore our moral responsibility we've always had towards one another and begin repairing the damage already caused to the country, the planet and people's lives, before the truly innocent members of society ever enter this realm of existence on planet Earth to begin living their lives more fully, always feeling safe and secure while doing so.

Once the good people of this nation realize that government can work alongside all citizens by providing greater opportunities and resources needed to bring about a greater sense of contentment in people's lives again then we may be able to finally end the needless division and distrust we show towards one another now and clearing a more harmonious pathway towards a brighter future so America can be envisioned ahead as The Greatest Nation on Earth.

Starting the process for change though is always the most difficult thing for most of us to do, which is why I'll continue my long-term efforts to advocate for much needed changes in Washington, but only when more Americans Take The Leap of Faith to provide the necessary support and start correcting the errors in judgement we've all made in the past for the sake of our children and generations to follow so their lives yet to be lived fully will not remain in such jeopardy as it does now, especially since the perils that lie ahead are through no fault of their own!

Our government, through its numerous outreach agencies once provided support and incentives for

America's citizens to explore new opportunities and take a chance on ways to live a more active and meaningful life ahead. Whether it was to start a business, enter into a career, or go to college to discover what your future aspirations may hold, agencies were there to provide some form of support as a means to an end, so those seeking a more inclusive and personally rewarding pathway forward in life could be given a chance to do so.

I remember when I started my own company in the early 1970's, after getting an AA Degree in Business Administration, the government SBA was there for me to help establish a line-of credit at my bank so I could have the funds available for operating expenses until the company could begin to sustain itself. They were anxious to provide any support they could to see me succeed when challenging my innovative spirit, contributing to the overall growth of the economy, but most importantly I would be starting a new enterprise that many viewed at the time as the founding principal for what we as a free society truly stood for. One's ambition leads to one's success then what follows innovation is heralded as 'made in America with pride.' Greed and self-preservation were not the prevailing attitudes in the society I grew up in. Unfortunately, today these are the main drivers behind an economy unable to move ahead and resume the lead in our rapidly changing global environment, that America once enjoyed as the leader in advancement and innovation, but now seen fallen 23 years behind other industrialized nations' that are moving far more progressively into the 21st century than we are yet to realize. Political leaders, specifically conservative members of Congress, have wasted our precious time on this planet far too long with their self-serving, counterproductive attitudes, doing nothing to incentivize young people to try and do any more or any less than they have in order to manage their day-to-day routine sufficiently.

Since members of Congress apparently report to no one except themselves and have no code of conduct for their performance on the job, it's now impossible to get the do nothing 'coasters' out, George Santos, Margery Taylor Green, Lauren Boebert, Matt Gaetz... since they are being evaluated by fellow partisan cohorts who have better things to do than rubber stamp their approval for those acting immorally and unethically throughout the continued dereliction of duty displayed while in office. But this disruptive and counterproductive behavior will only end once President Biden takes the necessary action that brings all members of Congress back to protecting and serving the needs of the people first and start addressing the critical issues the nation now faces, before the next interruption in all our lives takes us further away from ever returning to a semblance of safety and security throughout our homeland once more!

Hopefully over time as candidates running for the highest offices in the land will see little advantage being affiliated with a particular political group exclusively, allowing more challengers to enter the field as Independents because voters will now be electing their representatives to include the job and past performance qualifications required to hold such respectable positions in government going forward.

Speaking of Independent Candidates running for high offices, I actually campaigned for a run as 46th President of in the last election through change.org. Being self-funded and not really wanting the responsibility to clean up once again after the scorched earth remains were left behind by a previous Republican majority administration, I simply tried to gain support for much needed changes In America while We the People still had a voice in the decisions being made on our behalf in Washington. My pledge showed voters how much more secure and fulfilling their lives would be if this position was filled by someone focused solely on restoring our democracy back to the People's Republic that it was founded and envisioned to always move forward as one nation and evolve into a more perfect union! With only 200 plus supporters that I amassed during my run for presidency and election day now approaching rapidly, I sent out a message thanking all those who viewed and supported my thoughts and ideas on how to turn the country around before it moved further into darkness, to then ask everyone to now focus their undivided attention on electing Joe Biden as our next president.

I tried to highlight the critical juncture our nation remained motionless to ever move ahead again, hoping to convince more voters that we must never allow the highest office in the land to be filled by someone so incompetent and malevolent as the previous president turned out to be, showing how this could be our last best chance to restore pride and honor back in America ever again.

The rich American Way of Life has always remained ingrained in my human psyche, knowing our Republic was conceived to protect and serve the needs of the people unconditionally. To that end I continue to pay my fair share of taxes, giving back in causes designed to preserve the valuable resources that mankind no longer has any assurances will be maintained for future generations to try and sustain a more healthy and secure lifestyle as long as possible. I've only asked in return for my investments made in a country my family has called our homeland for over five generations, that the once enamored way of life found only in America is restored again.

Then future generations will be able to enjoy their lives more fully as I have always realized throughout mine, with guideposts in place that provide a more secure and inviting pathway ahead for young people to then follow the American Dream for themselves through: Life, Liberty and The Pursuit of Happiness, every step along the way.

There are many practical solutions still to be found if we ever hope to advance under one nation again. But until people's focus begins to shift away from continuing to be part of the core problem behind the country remaining in stasis today, perhaps we should just admit to ourselves that America has now become a Failed Experiment in Democracy and hope for the best going forward and try and prepare for the worst yet to come due to climate change growing more destructive to the environment year after year now!

Bringing manufacturing back to this country that creates more jobs we can then proudly purchase goods with the emblem "Made in America," is the first best step in stimulating the economy and providing a more equitable standard of living for everyone to live their lives with dignity. We have the resources, the technology and the labor force to be completely self-sufficient within our own borders. The only problem is we cannot afford to purchase our own goods at the current cost of labor and materials in this country alongside the unsustainable earnings distribution seen in the workplace. It is the huge disparity in salaries that has prevented all workers from earning at least a living minimum wage. As long as all workers are compensated a living wage and provided free access to healthcare while the cost to manufacture goods becomes more competitive, then more Americans can find good, higher paying jobs while enabling companies to compete on a global scale and become more profitable as a result. A win win scenario if only we weren't a nation driven by greed and disproportionate income distribution benefiting only those who continue to enrich their own lifestyles further simply because they can!

I have a solution that will stimulate manufacturing in this country, close the trade deficit and be able to become less dependent on foreign made goods to supply our insatiable need for material things. If the basic necessities to live a comfortable life were made available to everyone then discretionary spending would still flourish by everyone making an acceptable living wage. For individuals receiving greater compensation for their job performances consistently above and beyond the expectations listed in the job description, they would have the discretionary reserves to purchase those things considered luxury items to most people. Seniors remain an untapped resource who give migrant workers a run for their money, no pun intended, because of the ability to learn tasks quickly while expecting only modest compensation in return for their contributions to a productive workforce. Remember though sonny, we are good to go as long as there is no offset with our Social Security checks because of any additional earnings we may receive. Since the majority of the people now receiving government subsidies as welfare recipients are not totally disabled and can work in some capacity for their subsidy and/or housing allowance, then that becomes an untapped resource to stimulate the health of the economy in return. We could employ migrant workers, pay them a living wage as long as they have citizenship status or applied for citizenship in this country, to work in jobs other Americans choose not to do. Once we are able to lower labor costs, manufacture our own goods then more people will get jobs earning a living wage and be able to buy products "Made in America," instead of going outside our borders to support other economies.

I think an article written in the American Scholar by William Deresiewicz pretty much sums up one of the compelling reasons I am writing this book: "We have a crisis of leadership in America because our overwhelming power and wealth, earned under earlier generations of leaders, made us complacent, and for too long we have been training leaders who only know how to keep the routine going. Who can answer questions but do not know how to ask them. Who can fulfill goals but don't know how to set them. Who think about how to get things done, but not whether they're worth doing in the first place. What we have now are the greatest technocrats the world has ever seen, people who have been trained to be incredibly good at one specific thing, but who have no interest in anything beyond their area of expertise. What we don't have are people who can think for themselves, people who can formulate a new way of doing things, a new way of looking at things: people with vision. Introspection means talking to yourself, acknowledge things to yourself."

This attitude and way of thinking that surrounds true introspection as a means to assimilate greater knowledge and apply it in a meaningful way with everything we do in life, represents my own personal views to finding purpose in one's own existence on the planet.

As I said above, creativity and innovation are truly lacking in today's society. Our imaginations have been suppressed because those in power do not want us to think on our own. Their belief in mankind is that "a mind is a dangerous thing." Join me in proving them wrong and start to bring interest and innovation back into our lives during our brief time on this planet. Creativity and innovation are essential to be able to engage the younger generation and have them start to 'buy in' with making their lives purposeful on this planet. Creativity and innovation are essential to having a productive and collaborative workforce crossing all generational, gender and ethnic barriers. That is why I so firmly believe in focusing more on job creation through space exploration as a viable and attainable goal towards solving many of the inequities and shortcomings facing the current and future generation of thinkers and doers.

I reflect back on the ideas conceived in my own mind where I was able to turn linear thoughts into more tangible methods and find practical solutions that would allow me to problem solve more quickly and effectively around the challenges I decided to undertake. I once redesigned a more effective way to access perishable items stored deep in refrigerator cabinets that would expire from time to time because people lost sight of food products that became misplaced to the rear of the appliance and buried beyond view for months and years on end.

Then I came up with a modern design concept for space saving dinette sets where the four chairs with casters supporting the top would pivot in and out from under the table top making access to and from the modular piece of furniture very effective. The appliance manufacturers and modern furniture makers that I submitted detailed drawings to their design departments for review, never responded though, leaving me to assume outside ideas may have posed a threat to the design team's inability to come up with new and innovative concepts they were being paid to produce in house. Anyway, I guess that's just the sign of the times, where people are expected to no more or less than is absolutely necessary to get by in life and cover themselves in the workplace by accepting little responsibility beyond what you're told are the basic performance guidelines required just to keep your job.

Prologue

WHEN READING THE CAPTION BELOW THE PICTURE TO THE INTRODUCTION: PLEASE DON'T WAKE UP SOMEDAY TO REALIZE 'THE DREAMING TREE' A REFLECTION INTO YOUNG PEOPLES FUTURE, CAN NO LONGER BE REPLANTED ONTO THE SCORTCHED EARTH TERRAIN NOW LEFT BEHIND!

As I stated earlier... knowing the time I've already spent during this truly magical mystery tour of life, where my dreams and ambitions have been fulfilled beyond most people's wildest imagination, now makes this journey of mine on planet earth feel complete! Growing up in a generation where young people could live life more fully as free spirits doing what we were inspired to do without the needless distractions seen today coming out of Washington. We the People were promised mutual respect and compassion from our those we've always entrusted to protect and serve each of us unconditionally, honoring their positions as public servants to fulfill the needs of all citizens foremost.

I have watched in great dismay as the societal norms and attitudes have now shifted away from caring for one another to where people seem more focused on their own lives and wellbeing going forward today. Only as we begin to come out of isolation after the pandemic suspended everyone's way of life beyond a return to normalcy in familiar social surroundings, Will more people try and remember the way of life America has always been regarded where caring for one another in a time of need is the driving force behind equality born to us all in the human race. More than ever before in our nations evolutionary history as we move further into uncharted territory with so many challenges still left unresolved, leaves little time remaining to discuss the best course forward but how quickly we can now pull all our resources together and do what we can to save humanity beyond the errors in judgement we've all made in the past. Only then can we assure the truly innocent members of society they are not left alone to navigate through the perils that lie ahead with no safety nets in place when they need to reach out for a helping hand in a time of need.

I am hoping if nothing else is conveyed in the passages you've read in my manuscript so far, is that we will always overcome adversity in our own lives when we can unite as one, to look towards the future now, learning from the errors in judgement and mistakes we've all made in the past to never take the road leading nowhere again that we've now been traveling down long enough. Once we begin leading through the moral and ethical conscience ingrained in our human psyche and start to plan for a brighter future again in everyone's lives, only then will we be able to look into a child's eyes, telling them their pathway forward now looks more secure and inviting than ever before! Let's restore the pride in a way of life enshrined in the image America has always been seen as a country with the promise of Life, Liberty and The Pursuit of Happiness guaranteed for every man, woman and child to live their lives fully, as free spirits, the way I've always lived mine!

I was born gifted with the unique ability to problem solve ways around some of the most insurmountable challenges I've undertaken throughout my life so far when completing the tasks at hand my way, usually working through unconventional methods to bring forth practical and lasting solutions that allow me to meet and more often exceed my goals effectively and expeditiously each and every time. The practical knowledge I've assimilated places me in a position to formulate practical answers towards finding permanent solutions that more effectively begin addressing many of the challenges I've been faced in my own life, alongside ideas I have that will permanently fix most of what remains wrong in America today. But I can only offer practical solutions for this president to start taking a more aggressive approach through the powers he has been granted after he starts to address the core cause behind the continued dysfunction in government and try and salvage what remains of our once ingenious American way of life, while he still has the opportunity to do so.

I have now reached a stage in my life where there is nothing for me to personally gain or lose in the decisions people make today about their own future or loved one's fate now going forward, knowing that your continued silence is no longer an option if anyone else is concerned about the truly innocent members of society who will continue to inherit the untold challenges we've chosen once more to leave behind for them to navigate through alone, alongside the greatest threat to mankind already destroying the environment beyond repair through climate change.

OR

We can come together and work as one nation to try and save America, Planet Earth and return to a culture where we are guided by morality and restore hope in more people's minds towards a brighter future ahead once more, knowing you may even like the more positive transformation that takes place in your own lives again. I have personally become bored and disassociated with the antics being played out in Washington today by the bad actors in Congress where this once respected institution now holds the title as the worst reality show since the Apprentice that aired far past its continued low ratings reviews and should have been removed from public view sooner than it was.

The choice is still yours to make and I am willing and incentivized to continue along with my lifelong campaign advocating for ways to change course in America, but with my tenure on Planet Earth ending sooner than later now, I can only hope for the best outcome in people's lives from this day forward while looking inside my heart and soul and acknowledge to myself, at least I tried to change the self-destructive course humanity remains on today, even though no one else cared to do so!

I still believe today as I always have that there is inherit good in all mankind. We as humans are all a product of our upbringings and the environment in which we grew up in. Life for every living creature on this planet is truly about survival of the fittest. Even if you play by all the rules while exhibiting a spirit of compassion and generosity to those around you, there will always be some lost souls among us trying to take advantage of the good will we try and practice towards everyone alike. Those taking advantage of my caring spirit over the years and who perceived my honorable selfless intentions as a sign of weakness to be exploited for their personal gain, are hopefully in a better place somewhere in the universe by now. I am convinced that those with immense wealth and power for the most part, have taken advantage of the good people of this planet, only to further their insatiable quest for more wealth and power at the expense of society lacking the moral compass to differentiate between right and wrong when being told to take political sides over human interests firsts. The prevailing emotions driving the attitudes of people today seems to rests on fear and anger. People living in fear will always remain helplessly subservient to those in power. Those individuals focused solely on the self-serving quest for greater wealth and power can always rely on the weakness of others to further their own ambitions.

I would like to make the following plea to all the fine public service officials who took an oath of office to uphold the 'will of the people' first and foremost while in their positions in office: Internalize between right and wrong, good and evil and conclude as you must that the current 'rules of law' that provide the foundation for the attitudes and behavior necessary to maintain a free and democratic way of governance, are no longer in the image of our founding fathers and no longer work for those trying to live a more sustainable life with dignity.

Those tireless crusaders in Congress who have worked for the will of the people over any self or outside interests should stay the course knowing that help may be on the way if the American spirit, built on the care and compassion towards others, is awakened once again.

People today need not even question their moral convictions to understand that the drafters of the Articles of Freedom and Democracy reminded all of us that our duty as free citizens requires: whenever any *form of government* becomes destructive of these ends, it is the *right of the people* to alter or abolish it, and to institute new *government,* laying its foundation on such principals and organizing its powers in such form, as to them shall seem most likely to affect their *safety and happiness.*

The time has come to energize the progressives in this country and take a stand against all those trying to diminish the right of equality inherent in the American Way of Life. It is through a few, with their insatiable quest for greater wealth and power that if allowed to go unchecked, will ultimately turn this nation into an oppressive regime to which colonists escaped from that form of governance in Great Britain over four centuries ago. For those needing a party affiliation to move forward let's narrow it down to one, the party of "No More". No more suppressing the rights of the middle class. No more controlling the direction this country is moving without consent of the majority. No more manipulation of the truth by the media attempting only to highlight our weaknesses over our strengths. No more empty rhetoric without substantive dialogue to engage others to question the truth behind what is spoken. If you are unable to argue a case for your ideas then keep them to yourself. No more wasting our precious time on this planet with decision makers acting outside the interest of the majority of Americans. No more allowing one human being to inflict harm on another simply because they got away with it in the past.

Well saddle up and hold on for a wild ride elite and powerful. Take your material spoils you've acquired without compassion for the human suffering you have caused so many through your acts of unkindness. Vanish quietly from a society who no longer looks up to you as our once respected role models. I for one have paid my fair share of income taxes for many years during my career only to feel a deep sense of buyer's remorse today, when looking at the six-figure income that members of Congress receive while giving back little in return to taxpayers like myself who have always tried to coexist more harmoniously alongside my fellow Americans when trying to do the same.

I feel we have a share of ownership in America greater than that of the wealthy elite and corporations based here, because unlike those groups, most people respect their obligation to support a system that returns some of the proceeds back to its citizens. Unfortunately, most American's are feeling shortchanged today because the return on our investment with the government has become so marginal. I have always abhorred waste and frivolous spending by those who take little or no responsibility for paying their fair share into a system designed to benefit the majority of the people in this nation. Avoiding paying your fair share of income taxes just to purchase another vacation home does not constitute a humanitarian attitude towards your fellow mankind.

About The Author

Writing this book has afforded me an opportunity, for the first time in my life, to step back and reflect now on what an amazing experience life on planet Earth has been for me, from the moment I was transformed from the warm viscous environment I'd resided nine months prior to entering a more disorienting, dryer surrounds, feeling some physical discomfort that made me want to cry out loud, it quickly became real, wherever I had just landed was meant to be!

The sensory awareness feelings I had early in life, first physical then as my thought processes started to mature, seemed to kick into overdrive when I started to question in my mind, sights and sounds I was introspectively thinking whether they made sense in that context of perception or needed more thought-provoking review before being filed away in the archives of my brain. I remember asking my mom in my youth, what actually happened on that eventful moment I Fell to Earth when feeling some physical discomfort and being disoriented when the doctor started whooping me for no reason, I could think of except perhaps his holiday plans on January 1st were cut short when having to come into work and help deliver me into my new surroundings in Texas of all places to land!

As I started to mature both physically and mentally, I remember asking the adults in the room, questions why things were the way I was perceiving them in my mind before it finally got to a point when my grandmother said to me, "Johnny you should be seen and not heard from so much," which lead me to immediately ask what she meant by that? The silence in the room became deafening after that!

The curiosity about this new life I'd entered into was in constant motion where sights and sounds alongside my emotions were being tested and leading me to try and formulate in my mind if things made sense to me.

Then everything started to change once I was told in early adolescence, I'd be facing many challenges in my life trying to adapt in a more disciplined manner with the learning disorder I had that the medical community simply labeled as Dyslexia. Unfortunately, with very little medical research being done around my condition at that time to help me navigate through the uncertain times ahead and my parents unsure what they could do to help, then left me to try and problem solve life's challenges from that point forward on my own!

When told the mental disorder I had would limit my ability to focus long term and comprehend what was being taught in a classroom environment, soon evolved into a gift in life that allowed me to formulate ideas and concepts in my own mind through a more linear and progressive way of thinking to arrive at answers on how best to keep moving ahead. That then allowed me to problem solve even the most insurmountable challenges that I faced, always finding practical solutions to continue towards the end goal I set out to achieve when doing so beyond all expectations, including my own.

I also found out later that there was a social disconnect associated with Dyslexic individuals when carrying on a conversation where the thoughts I was trying to verbalize were sometimes misconstrued by those listening to what I was saying. I initially thought that it was because my family moved so often making it difficult for me connect with friends long-term so they could provide feedback when I spoke my thoughts out loud that may not have been interpreted by others the way I meant the words to come out more cohesively.

It seems like through my entire life, during every waking moment my mind was like a sponge absorbing practical knowledge and information I could continue to assimilate when by getting out in the real world and experiencing what other people were doing in their lives thinking ahead it may be something I'd want to pursue myself someday.

I started traveling early in my adult life touring across America and Canada with the person who would soon become a soulmate and life partner alongside me, for us to begin exploring together, all that life had to offer when stepping out of each of our familiar surroundings to see what adventures may still lie ahead as a couple. The van we were traveling in was something you would see out of a Hollywood movie set when starting to explore my more artistic side with the creations I made usually out of wood that turned into one-of-a-kind furniture pieces and later architectural features I would place in the home built as a labor of love in the Redwoods above Los Gatos. This mobile homestead we were traveling in was outfitted with a couch that folded out into a bed, stained glass windows, a stove top and sink mounted to a tile countertop that pivoted on the rear doors to cook and clean up outside. I even outfitted the cockpit with seats taken out of a 707-passenger jetliner that was no longer in service I was told. After those road trips were taken, I went on to satisfy my insatiable curiosity about what there was still to view and reflect on once visiting other continents around the globe when doing so scuba diving only where aquatic creatures have roamed before, on land hiking through towns and paths in the surrounding terrain and high atop mountain ranges reaching the crests and looking out past the vast expanses wondering what life was like in those remote locations as far as the eye could see.

By the time I'd reached early adulthood and continuing to take full control my future plans in life through the decisions I had made and ability to overcome the challenges I'd already faced by now, allowed me to take the leap of faith and begin a career track that opened the door to new opportunities that I became excited and anxious to then pursue. While in the initial stages of getting my business up and running, I took on a project that entailed homesteading a piece of land in a rural community before breaking ground to start construction of our future dream home, initially with no utilities in the area, making this venture even more challenging than I ever imagined. I spent the next twenty-five years growing a successful enterprise alongside building a beautiful home as I learned how to complete the work requirements associated with the various building trades myself. I studied local code requirements to be in compliance with the county planning guidelines, usually building above and beyond local standards since I was doing most of the work myself. I knew the entire project would be completed code compliant that provided me the confidence to build without no stinkin permits along the way should I ever go before the building departments tribunal and have to confess my sins to them knowing then I could prove the structure was engineered and built far above county standards at that time. Hey, I was from the generation where we objected to authority telling us what to do as free spirits when the decisions we made came from a 'higher and higher' order we received guidance from, usually after two hits were taken from joints we assembled with tops only, no stems or seeds thank you!

After a quarter century of following my life's dreams and ambitions where my once thriving enterprise was shuttering due to a technology shift towards PC computing and the home I had built was completed and permitted after the fact at great expense, made me realize the time was now to move forward and begin pursuing other avenues of interest that still awaited my discovery. Since I had gotten very proficient in the building trades, I decided to test my construction skills in a commercial setting, going on to build a retail space, warehouse and animal boarding facility for a couple who wanted to expand their business further onto the three-acre parcel of land they lived within the city limits. I also began remodeling the home we moved into closer to town that needed many upgrades to bring it up to the standards we had grown accustomed to in the previous dwelling I built. I then taught myself how to create landscaping features such as koi ponds and waterfalls that became focal points of interests for people driving by on the way to Monterey Bay beaches nearby.

After that I decided to test the waters for the first time in my career to go to work under the supervision of someone other than myself. At first as a Home Services Manager for a company providing Weatherization Measures to low-income customers renting the residences that needed to be retrofitted with energy saving materials to lower their utility bill. I taught crews how to install new home heating units alongside solar applications for more efficient water heaters in the homes we worked on, doing so as I had always done in the past, through the introspective knowledge I had assimilated over time providing me the ability to problem solve the way I knew would be the most efficient and effective way possible in compliance for the most part, with any professional or government standards required should inspections ever be made and approval needed to sign off on the project as complete.

I got licensed after that to administer health and life policies to groups seeking insurance coverage for their employees when entering a new field for me as Customer Service Manager with a woman owned and run Insurance Brokerage Firm. All I can say is let the force be with you gals, knowing now what women have had to endure a more inequitable workplace environment far too long when their employer is a male owned/run business.

So that's enough about me other than to say I don't believe you have to be born into this life with the gift I've been given to choose your own destiny at any time during the brief passage we all have before us here on Earth. Instead of waiting for someone else to tell you what they feel is in their own best interest for you decide what still lies ahead in your life yet to be discovered fully, I urge everyone to take the leap of faith now and begin fulfilling the dreams and ambitions you've always wanted to pursue knowing there are no guarantees in life what tomorrow may bring?

I've never slowed down long enough until now to question how one person could accomplish as much as I have in the short time, I've been able to do so, by completing the work myself and the tasks at hand my way, realizing success each and every time beyond all expectations! It just goes to show how much potential we have as mortal human beings to challenge ourselves starting with the simple thought in our minds why not try change, knowing greater meaning and purpose can come into your life during the brief time we all have to experience the limitless opportunities that still lie ahead.

Thinking back, if I can accomplish as much as any one person on earth could do so by themselves, with the mental disorder I was told would present so many untold challenges ahead for me to try and manage on my own, just think of the possibilities for young people today, if you are ready and willing to take chances in life in Pursuit of the American Dream the way it was described to me in: The belief that anyone, regardless of where they were born, or what class they were born into, can attain their own version of success in a society in which upward mobility is possible for everyone in this Republic that America was chartered, where We the People are the ultimate decision makers to choose our own destiny during our residency here on Planet Earth!

I can only hope some of the passages contained in my book will arouse your awareness to the fact that we are only given the opportunity once in this lifetime to live a full and more meaningful existence during our brief passage here on Planet Earth. So, I urge you not to waste another precious moment in time and get out there to begin your own magical mystery tour of life as I have always enjoyed, knowing you may even like the amazing transformation that now beholds you going forward where no man, woman or child has gone before!

After I convince the president to the urgency with which he must act now to finally end the needless distractions in Washington then and only then will all Americans be able to focus their undivided attention towards the future and never looking on the most insecure and vulnerable position we lie in today, now waiting for the worst yet to come through climate change!

THE BEGINNING!

www.ingramcontent.com/pod-product-compliance
Lightning Source LLC
LaVergne TN
LVHW022000060526
838201LV00048B/1636